BECAUSE SADNESS IS BEAUTIFUL?

Poems

Tanaka Chidora

Edited by Tendai R. Mwanaka

Mwanaka Media and Publishing Pvt Ltd,
Chitungwiza Zimbabwe
*
Creativity, Wisdom and Beauty

Publisher: Mmap

Mwanaka Media and Publishing Pvt Ltd

24 Svosve Road, Zengeza 1

Chitungwiza Zimbabwe

mwanaka@yahoo.com

www.africanbookscollective.com/publishers/mwanaka-media-and-publishing

https://facebook.com/MwanakaMediaAndPublishing/

Distributed in and outside N. America by African Books Collective

orders@africanbookscollective.com

www.africanbookscollective.com

ISBN: 978-1-77929-596-5

EAN: 9781779295965

DISCLAIMER

All views expressed in this publication are those of the author and do not necessarily reflect the views of *Mmap*.

i

ii

Dedication

To Villes, Josh and Stephanie, the people around whom my life revolves

ACKNOWLEDGEMENTS

In 2018, I spent a weekend with David Mungoshi, Memory Chirere, Ignatius Mabasa, Philani Nyoni, Mercy Dhliwayo, Karolina Jeppson, Goran Goransson and other literature enthusiasts from Sweden.. I watched David, Memory, Mercy and Philani read and perform their poems and I said to myself, "Damn! This is cool!" A few weeks later, Mbizo Chirasha gave me space for my first poem, 'Magamba Hostels', in his Brave Voices journal. That did it! The padlock that had kept poetry trapped inside was broken at last.

David and Memory went on to read my manuscript and recommend certain changes that helped in shaping this collection to what it is today. Many a morning, Ignatius Mabasa would say, "The way you are writing young man…" A comment of that nature from a literary guru of Ignatius Mabasa's standing helped in building my confidence.

During my first tottering steps as a poet, the Zimbabwe Historical Association Whatsapp group became the slate on which I wrote some of my early pieces. And oh, how they read them! How they encouraged me to continue writing! Edward Dzonze and the Poetry Intercourse Whatsapp group, Khumbulani Muleya and the Gourd of Consciousness Whatsapp Group, Zimbabwe Writers Association Whatsapp Group, UZ Department of English and Media Studies Whatsapp Group, Harare Book Club Whatsapp Group, Writing Issues Whatsapp Group, and the wonderful Mudakuvaka Family Whatsapp Group all provided platforms for me to write my poems and be groomed, through their gentle feedback, into the poet that I am today.

My poetry mate, Millicent Yedwa, with whom I am writing something that does not have a name, something that is even strange to us, I am grateful for the long discussions we had concerning poetry, and for availing your inbox to me to use as a creative slate. Batsirai

Chigama encouraged me to get the poems out there and even sent me to my first photoshoot. I am grateful.

Tendai Rinos Mwanaka, we met on Facebook, and by the time we met face to face in the dusty streets of Zengeza, you had already read my manuscript and suggested changes that made it not only a collection of poems, but a narrative, a map, of a country, a person, a life. I am forever grateful for your patience in guiding me through the whole process of publishing this collection.

Magdalena Pfalzgraf, for reading my manuscript and writing such a beautiful foreword, I am indebted to you. I value your friendship. And I want to confess that there are moments when I really miss oysters. They are part of my memory of Frankfurt.

To my Facebook readers, your Likes and Comments spurred me on. I love you to bits.

Table of Contents

Walking cities, conquering pavements: foreword to Tanaka Chidora's *Because Sadness is Beautiful?*

In 2014, I had the opportunity to spend a couple of weeks as a visiting doctoral researcher in the English Department of the University of Zimbabwe in Harare. My Zimbabwean colleagues were hospitable and generous. They included me in the different teaching and research activities in the department and ensured that my stay would be productive and enjoyable. Tanaka Chidora was then a young lecturer in the department whose teaching included diverse and varied areas such as contemporary popular cultures (in particular the ZimDancehall genre, of which he is an expert), Postcolonial Theory, Theories of Literature, and Zimbabwean literature. We chatted on the department floors and over tea in Portia's secretary's office, and I was grateful to him for showing me around Harare and opening up the city to me beyond the campus and academic conversations.

When he called himself jokingly the "connoisseur of Harare", I laughed, but I soon understood how apt this was. I once returned the joke by calling him Harare's secret mayor, because he knew about all sorts of cultural events going on and places to go, and he seemed to know people everywhere. He also displayed a peculiar ability to be in several places at the same time, often making surprise appearances or turning up late, grand-entry style. Our friendship was aided by the fact that we were both about a year or so into our PhDs and that we shared an interest in representations of movement in post-2000 Zimbabwean writing. Tanaka wrote a thesis on exile in post-2000 Zimbabwean literature, mine focused on mobility in Zimbabwean post-2000 fiction, so in fact, we had two options: murder the other or jump into the same trench and work together (I wish to stress that my attempt to instill a love for oysters in Tanaka a few years later was entirely innocent).

Early on in his life, Tanaka became a practitioner of what Beck termed place polygamy. Born in 1985 in Rukovo, a village south of the city of Masvingo in southern Zimbabwe, he moved to Harare as a teenager to complete his secondary school education at Mount Pleasant High School. The unhurried life of the village and vast expanses of space that would remain visible to the eye up to that point where mountains met the sky undoubtedly influenced Tanaka's keen sense of observation which comes out more succinctly where Tanaka describes places and people's relationships to them.

In the city, attachments to places multiplied and maps became more complex as Tanaka commuted daily from his aunt's home in Magaba Hostels (which in his writing appears as Magamba Hostels) in Mbare (Harare's oldest and dirtiest ghetto) to Mount Pleasant High School. This continued throughout his university years at the University of Zimbabwe, whose campus is located near Mount Pleasant High School, between 2005 and 2012. For his PhD, he travelled back and forth between the University of the Free State in South Africa and Harare where he continued to teach in the English Department at the University of Zimbabwe. It hence comes as no surprise that Tanaka's debut collection of poetry is so concerned with tracing the particulars of place. Reading the poems chronologically, a journey unfolds and topographies unveil as the poet captures a variety of different Zimbabwean locales on the page. Tanaka's poetry appeals to all senses.

We get to hear, feel, even taste and smell the places which unfold in an almost three dimensional way as we travel through the collection and through Zimbabwe. The poetry takes us to Masvingo, to Mbare, inside Magamba Hostels and other houses. We are moving level on the ground, "under sagging roofs" and inside "wooden structures", we are following a protagonist "to the house at the end of the street", curious to find out what will happen next. And then the perspective changes, and country and city are viewed from above.

The collection also gives us a glimpse and speculation on how the author's perspective has evolved. There is the comfort of the child's contained, trusting vision, the detached, critical view of country life and of the city, the clear expression of political critique: "A broken grin is my response//to the propaganda of these arrogant shits//who want to show me the way//to a promised land that keeps drifting further away". Most poems engage very distinctly with Zimbabwe's political and social realities, but this does not mean that they are not easily accessible to a wider readership. In fact, Tanaka's biting humor often speaks to everyone who is human in this world and able to relate to "unwanted farts", which feature prominently in the collection, or to the "the purging power of shit". That Tanaka is not afraid of raised eyebrows or sharp intakes of breath does not surprise me at all, as I have seen Tanaka speak at conferences where he was not intimidated by seniority or afraid to ruffle a few feathers.

He even stood his ground when he was once accused by an elderly professor of being "one of those young people who want to be like Europeans". In his debut collection, Tanaka has developed his own voice as a poet, but he also acknowledges a wider tradition by allowing famous, canonised Zimbabwean writers to speak (such as Dambudzo Marechera), and by including numerous subtle nods to younger writers; readers recognise Bulawayo's *We Need New Names* in the reference to "guava-speckled excrement" and to Lawrence Hoba's *The Trek and Other Stories* in "the creaky oxcart".

We now look back on six years of warm, firm friendship and a most fruitful scholarly cooperation. We have kept an open conversation and exchange about our research alive despite the geographical distance. There have been visits to conferences, extended Whatsapp conversations, exchanges of written drafts, and honest opinions. Returning Tanaka's hospitality and welcoming him to Frankfurt in 2018 was a great pleasure. As we walked along the river Main in sunshine, we engaged in a heated discussion about whether Harare or Frankfurt was the larger or more sprawling city. Tanaka's argument was that Frankfurt felt more extensive out whereas he felt that he could draw the map of Harare in the centre of his palm. I felt that the opposite was true, and argued that it needed a few more walks on Frankfurt's pavements, and then it would fit into his palm just as easily. I am sure that readers will be grateful to Tanaka for inviting them on a walk through Harare and other places in Zimbabwe and develop their own maps because, as he once said, "we conquer cities by walking on their pavements", but I think art can also help us to feel them on the page.

Magdalena Pfalzgraf, Saarland University

there is a country whose main pre-occupation
is to allocate sadness to its people

opening lines

the ugly underbelly of the new
reveals itself to a few.

silence's yawning black hole
is an omen of what is in store.

they have gathered these bits and pieces
into the emperor's unconvincing treatise.

the rising sun smiles upon the world
but the smile reveals the clandestine gathering of the old.

they raise passionate fists into the air
but some of the fists do not make a pair.

the weather is unusually fine
but the same cannot be said about the time.

"I took my things and left"1
but not before pissing on freedom's cleft.

---

1 I consider this line by Dambudzo Marechera (*The House of Hunger*,
1978: 1) the coolest opening line I have ever come across in a novel,
besides Jose Saramago's in *Death and Intervals* (2005).

armed peace
(to Wesley Mwatwara)

sitting here on this tranquil precipice
and looking at that jutting rock
that looks like a witch's scythe,

reminds me of a country whose peace
is patrolled by beasts, bullets and bayonets,

reminds me of sitting near a serene river
whose serenity sits astride the jaws of a leviathan,

reminds me of a peace armed to the teeth
and a fetid silence hovering above Lucifer's cemetery,

reminds me of that smile
whose jacket is festooned with untruths,

reminds me of the deranged storm
hiding in Sunlight's skirts,

reminds me of the hideous stain
hiding beneath the elegant surface of a legacy,

reminds me of this:
the old that hides in the folds of the new.

forgotten doubles
(to Sudan, from a Zimbabwean)
7 August 2019

there are paths that we walk
that carry the familiarity of past paths
so that you have these thoughts
that stalk the terrains of your mind
making you suspect the mischief of hallucination
or the recklessness of inebriation
when your mind questions you:
have we not been here before?

my nostalgia makes me miss the past
even though it was an interminable fast
of empty bellies and empty shelves,
crying widows and unfathered orphans,
desperate acts and berserk nerves,
corrupt politicians and missing funds.

now I look at the present
and shudder at the past's effrontery
to rebirth itself in the present
depriving me of joy's pristine confectionery
and making me ask myself why there is a new dispersion
at a time when I am being told of the new dispensation.

the 3pm field inspection
(Zimbabwe, November 2018)

the squirming earth meets the old men's feet
but his feet meet it with trepidation.
the toes…
his toes are the voice
 that cries in the wilderness,
"It comes not! It comes not!"

but even as the voice cries,
the deafening silence of the world
that sighs and squirms and turns
silently, stoically,
swallows the voice in the wilderness
and lets it reverberate in the wrinkles of its insides,
"It comes not! It comes not!"

the silence:
the wind has nothing to rustle
except the frayed ends
of the old man's overalls,
the river has no seductive invitation
for the squeal of a girl
whose firm breasts have been tickled
by the water's hefty belch
released timeously to receive her naked body.

the silence:
it speaks,
it speaks of huts
that no longer crown themselves

with the afternoon smoke
of breathing fireplaces
and sighing pots

the beginning is back
because he has three legs now
soon they will be four.

in the beginning there was,
in the end there will be

the beginning

but this beginning is very strange:
it has no movement in the compound,
it has no libidinous cockerel
to chase mischievous hens,
it has no drum
and no handwriting
on the base of a laden sky.

the voice that cries in the wilderness,
"They come not! They come not!"
is swallowed into the wrinkles of the silence.

the silence:
the air has no hopeful messages
of the first and second coming
for the first coming has heeded
the message of the changing times
and the second coming has heeded
the message of the times that have not changed.

a tale of two writers
(To Dambudzo Marechera and Charles Mungoshi)

on this teapot-shaped piece of earth
two writers once walked and took their breaths
and scribbled on it ominous foretales
of dreams and visions that will hang, stale
in the dead autumn airs that will forever hang
like a witch's sceptre over the country's denizens.

Dambudzo squirmed under the house of hunger in his mind
a hunger that mercilessly ate the shrivelled bellies of mankind.
he took the hunger and transmogrified it
into a confectionery of pleasure that lit
the minds of the young whose fiery rhymes
are now the voices that fly in the wind to scythe
the rhetoric of the beast that lords over us.

Charles looked at the abandoned and rusty scotch-cart
and it conjured an image that made him start:
an accusing finger at the empty sky,
an accusing finger from a junk-heap that continues to sigh
while waiting in abeyance for a Lazarus drop to stop this vice
of the dry throats of the ancestors and dry memories of their
children,
an accusing finger to a dusty sky
which, in the place of tears, wrings tattered underwear in reply.

on this teapot-shaped piece of earth
two writers scribbled with their pens
the breadth and depth of the fate
of those who wait and hunger for
a home that is home no more,
a home whose children wear tired grins

7

while the beast drowns its conscience in the gin
that is purchased with rivers of blood.

one day I wrote about this place
(to Binyavanga Wainana)

one day I wrote about this place
about how, if I had asked you
to paintbrush a description of it,
I would expect crazy strokes
quarrelling for space on shredded canvas,
about how the hand that held the paintbrush
quarrelled with the head that conceived the idea,
about how the paint and the bucket
decided to settle matters by lying on loose grains of sand.

one day I wrote about this place
about how autumn airs hung forever
above the sagging roofs under which we were housed,
roofs that sagged under the weight of a lethargic sky,
roofs that sagged under the weight of rotting autumn leaves
until those who lived under the roofs
shrank back into themselves to die silently.

one day I wrote about this place
about how silence brooded over it
and how the whispers that were heard in the wind
were only of silence conversing with the phantoms in his head,
phantoms of the dead whose stories

had disappeared in silence's folds
to echo in those folds, untold.

one day I wrote about this place
about the bizarre handwriting on the people's faces,
records of desperation extending from their faces
to hang above the city like a network of neon bulbs
hung up by a disinterested Christmas artist.

Magamba Hostels
(to my unborn novel)

wooden structures mushroom in the night
jostle for space towards dawn
and, in the morning, present a motley sight
that tells the story of those who spawn
hope
                    then dust.

the walls that house me…
they have dark sockets during the day
and at night, dark sockets and night
become the brooding silence that will stay
until another hiccup
of hope
                    then dust.

we live on as stories that will be told
long after we are dead and gone
but here, we live in silence's folds
brooding, sighing silently like Stone
with broken moments
of hope
                    then dust.

I cannot escape in the city lights
the curse of Stone for whom I bear a name
for the wind that howled in the night
and left ruinous glory and fame
is here, howling
howling away my hope
and leaving nothing in its wake
                    but dust

the things I carry

some of the things are measurable
in terms of lengths, weights, heights;
some are just immeasurable
like love, hatred, fright;
others, life-threatening
like when you carry a whole country
and your back forgets the joys of straightening
and you too forget what it means to write poetry
because the hands that are meant to arrange words
are wiping away the tears that accompany your sobs.

slow country

the dreary days drag by
exuded by austerity's world,
a garbage of desperation on their backs.

the slow and laborious progress of the days
reminds me of the birthing agonies
of guava-speckled excrement toiling against
the contractions of the rectum's folds.

during the day, the sun's smile suffers a still birth
from the torments of breathing in dust-speckled air,
and during the night
the moon's energies fail to quench
the insatiable demands of the darkness
that broods over the silent landscapes of the slow country.

the skeletal fingers of the cold grope in the darkness
for human prey to munch through the night
and we fold our bodies into an assortment of shapes
in an attempt to keep the cold at bay
but the cold, undeterred by our vain re-creations of self,
licks our skins slowly and thoughtfully
like a python lubricating its prey
before the slippery passage of the great feast
into its unforgiving belly.

night gives way to morning
to the shock of an unchanged world,
to the trauma of surviving a single day's assault on the mind,
to the thirst that flaunts itself at our throats,
and to the extended growls that convert our stomachs
into frightening lion kingdoms.

waiting
(To Joseph Mujere)

time stands mischievously
nodding slightly
like a recalcitrant erection;
our delight is in standing
because standing means
we may perhaps move –

backwards
forward
sideways
up and down.

this facility where time is frozen
like chunks of butchered limbs
is a home to me;
there are other homes
that I carry in my head,
but this home, this facility,
is the one my feet tread on.

so I am here with my feet;
I am in my head too –
moving, standing
standing, moving

backwards
forward
sideways
up and down,

a patient of the state.

to the seven
(born in Zimbabwe)

Sunday,
you have always been the religious one,
the one to raise undefiled hands heavenwards
as sweet incense to the force that stays in our hearts,
the force of faith, hope and love,
the force that kept us trudging on
even when we knew the tragedy of our irrelevance here.

Monday,
many people approached you with trepidation
because your presence was an omen
of more days distending before us
like the remaining thirty-nine of a wilderness fast;
you Monday, vanquished the hope, faith and love of Sunday
with the clatter and arrogance of your demands upon us.

Tuesday,
you have always been the ordinary one,
indifferent like the touch of fingers on a lover's numb cheeks;
you did not announce your presence
like someone afraid of knowing herself,
so we saw you, walked a little with you
and forgot that you were once with us.

Wednesday,
you have always been the deceptive one
and your attempts to put on Friday's garish apparel
usually invited a couple of dancers to serenade you
until they discovered the lie hidden in your loud hips
before reluctantly leaving you alone

while muttering apologetically, we are really sorry,
it's Friday we are looking for.

Thursday,
you and Tuesday shared a lot in common:
someone could meet Wednesday and Friday
and still forget that another sibling had been bypassed;
of course you were more tolerable than Monday
because you were not an omen of days stretching ahead like a
nightmare;
you were merely a reminder that Friday was around a corner.

Friday,
oh my Friday!
you have always been the spoiled one,
jumping on a lover's lap and showering him with kisses
while giggling the night away,
and in turn the lover would shower you with gifts
and give you the keys to the city,
that endless conglomeration of lights and sites
until Saturday's impatient knock
for the lover's famous attentions.

Saturday,
always been the fragile one,
you loved to sleep late into the day
and complained about the dull throb in your head
and said you felt like a maniacal drummer resided in there;
you would spend the whole day wishing
that Friday had not duped you into taking one too many
but regret is more painful than sin
so you would fling the nagging thought aside
and nurse your throbbing head
while coaxing the drummer to relent.

but these days, you my seven are all the same;
you stretch ahead of me like a forty-day fast
with your shrivelled buttocks and withered thighs
that have ceased to awaken my flaccid phallus
to fantasies of a seven day orgy;
now each of you comes and goes
like an eternal curse pronounced by a sadistic god;
the dreary days stretch before my eyes
like a vast apocalyptic wasteland;
I cannot give you life
for the force that has frozen time
is here, freezing my faith, hope and love.

silence
(after Zimbabwe's infamous internet shutdown)

silence's overcoat
stifling the squirms
of those who live
under its suffocating stench,

silence's cold hands
caressing the wasteland
whose dimples are the pools
of gangrene welling
from the diseased bodies
of its undead,

now silence is…

shut the fuck up!!!

the dying city

she has things crawling inside her
inside the morsels of reason that she has left,
they crawl around her
aimlessly,
desperately,
sickly things with tired grins.

her parted thighs are the mouth of the stream,
the stream that carries her future foetuses
to the puddle of putrefaction that lies downstream
where her former glitz and glamour sit at the bottom
like ancient artefacts of a forgotten civilisation.

around her, spires of former glory
point skeletal fingers at a vacant sky
while the eyes of the head from which the spires protrude
stare at the hollowness of the wasteland
on which she forlornly sits.

silence stalks the wasteland
with double-edged machetes
to slice through the heads of sound
that sprout above the garbage of the wasteland
from the hovels of the past and the future.

the dying city is this emaciated body,
this unclothed landscape
of women,
of men,
of children,
of a generation that has found itself
in an apocalyptic wasteland

of dead dreams and comatose visions.

this old country
(To Sibanengi Ncube)

this country used to be young and sprightly
like a young boy creating heaven-bound spirals
of urine shooting from a turgid phallus
for young voyeurs to watch and cheer.

but now, like an old prostate-ridden phallus,
the heaven-bound spirals are gone
and in their place is a lazy trickle
that timidly kisses the ground
with the stealth of wounded lips.

sounds

the drum used to roll here
its sound echoing far and near
to cuddle hearts full of fear,
to remind us even when the skies were clear
that rain would fall again,
that the swish-swish of grazing cattle
would once again serenade our afternoons.

on this ground trees used to grow
and from them the sound of the crow
would quicken the legs of the slow
and give to dark spirits a glow
that would light the future
and give to it a glorious halo
for pathfinders to greet from afar.

on this homestead children used to abound
in shirttails they would run around
inviting generous rain with the sound
of yelling and shouting to astound
even the stingiest of gods
into releasing their tears
as relief for the scorched earth.

now, the drum is gone,
the trees and crows are gone,
the children are gone.

in their place is the sound of gunshots,
the sound of a wailing mother
staring at a bloodied bundle lying in her arms,
the sound of a dusty storm raising its head

like an angry snake on this desolate plain,
the sound of running feet,
the sound of gun butts connecting with skulls,
the sound of tired sighs that fly in the wind...

these sounds
and melancholic whispers
are what's left of what used to be.

austere days

there are days when my thoughts
gather at a corner and share a joint
or argue about how to plot
the bearer's path on this dusty soil.

the joint makes them laugh
and slap each other's shoulders
for taking the obstinate and tough
and turning it into fodder
for thoughts to munch on for days.

then there are other days
when there is no joint to share
and each thought limbs away
to an obscure corner somewhere
to lick the wounds of austerity's assault
on the bare backs of tired thoughts.

a broken grin

a broken grin is my response
to the propaganda of these arrogant shits
who want to show me the way
to a promised land that keeps drifting further away
like the elusive breath-taking climax
that the phallus keeps looking for.

a broken grin is this old country
whose khaki overalls hide a diseased body
above which hovers a chorus of flies,
retching, eating, retching, eating
the gangrene that flows from its body,
balm for the sadists who weave curses with fists.

a broken grin is the filth that is thrown in the rain
after being ransacked out by calloused hands
that are eager to clean the house at the beast's bidding
for the feast of the maidens and the beast
and the earth-shattering groans of the beast
as it releases baptismal fluid into the bottles
that sit forlornly between splayed thighs.

a broken grin is this crowd of minute skeletons of revelation
that fumbles its skeletal way
into the hungry wombs of these dirty bodies,
the minute skeletons that become seeds
that sprout out to become legs and heads
that carry the burden of the revelation
with a fervour that makes Sisyphus but a mere toddler.

a broken grin is,
                finally,

        me,
peering in the shimmering heat of the wasteland
for that cloudy hand
that bears the promise of rain.

portrait of a policeman's gumboot connecting with shrivelled buttocks

the policeman's body slants to the left
like a eucalyptus bending to the rage of the wind,
but the policeman is not bending to rage;
he is bending with a puppet's rage,
a rage that contorts his face into premature aging,
a rage that drives his boot
against the shrivelled buttocks of his mother
against the shrivelled buttocks of his father
against the shrivelled buttocks of his grandmother
against the shrivelled buttocks of his grandfather.

the protester's body strains against the prohibition of age
but age and rage sabotage her flight
and deliver her body on a silver platter
for the policeman's boot to ravage.

the boot that carries the rage of the system
descends on vulnerable bones,
bones that are already creaking under the assault of austere days
and the cracking sound of bones
suddenly opens the protester's eyes
to the hovering presence of death,
a presence that bulks small
the protester's grievances against the system
because in death, you are alone
even in the midst of stampeding feet.

the death of Vanda

the police!
they are coming this way!
that muzzle is pointing at us!
they are shooting!
RUN!!

is that tear gas?
yes, it is!
look! They are throwing it!
look!
RUN!!

soldiers!
they are coming this way!
they are shooting too!
RUN!!

use colgate! Use colgate!
on the nose!
but don't stop!
RUN!!

where is Vanda?
where did Vanda go?

he's running!
just RUN!!

are you sure Vanda is running?

he was running with us!
he was here!

but where is he now?

VANDA!
VANDA!
VAAAAAANDA!!!!
VANDAAAAAAAAAA!!!!!

the missing childhood

I have been looking for my childhood
carefully parting the shrubs in the woods
with the hope that I might have left it
lying carelessly like a used condom in the midday heat.

I have been looking for my childhood
scouring the dumpsite like a dog searching for food,
like a village madman looking for a pie chart
to brandish before a dumbfounded teacher and his class.

I have been looking for my childhood
scrutinising, like a girl inspecting the chest for an elusive boob,
the school's dusty playground
hoping to turn the dusty story into some lost and found.

I have been looking for my childhood
scratching underneath my desperate mood
until the silent whispers in the wind told me:
my childhood was last seen disappearing
into the underbrush that lay beyond the 80s clearing,
the underbrush of the 90s, 2010s and 2020s,
the underbrush of scary nightmares and frivolous daydreams.

tunnel walls
(to Mandiedza Parichi)

open your eyes and see
that there is nothing to see,
that this pervasive wall of darkness
has become taller and longer
and that various patterns left by tender foreheads
connecting with stonewalls
give to the walls the adornment
of a bizarre artist's brush strokes
running berserk against stone.

open your ears to hear
that there is nothing to hear
except voices whizzing past
in the darkness of the tunnel,
desperate voices,
hysterical voices,
voices trying in vain to breach
the claustrophobics of the tunnel
only to bounce back and whizz
towards another wall,
another attempt,
before flopping to the floor
to be shrouded in the tunnel's darkness.

take a step
forward?
backwards?
does it matter, really?
the sensation of planting your feet

on the nothingness of darkness is the same
and the panic that opens wide your eyes
is yours alone to feel,
because in the darkness of the tunnel
you are alone.

independence
(18 April 2019)

trepidation whips the buttocks of my joy.
timid heads of the future peep from home's bloodied soil
and quickly sink back after sniffing trouble in the air.
my knuckles hurt from punching the iron face of Blair
and my flag…

the red on it has grown bigger,
the black is speckled with white blisters,
and my blinkered vision cannot help me tell
why the green on the flag has become pale.

I smoke to herald independence's entrance.
I smoke and puff until, caught in a trance,
and with a keener eye for truths untold,
I see her in chains, cold
raped by villains in shining armour.

flame

independence's flame burns in the rain
and licks the drops that are supposed to take away our pain.

there's flames everywhere;
the mouth of the gun spits some
to fry those who want hope to come.

and when brothers put food on the table for little babies
the tables go up in smoke before they know it.

the preacher's mouth is spewing fire and brimstone
to shrivel the skins of sinners whose hearts are like stone.

so when we want to call fire to burn these maggots
there is no fire left; except this stubborn...
this incorrigible bastion of those who steal the fire!

freedom fighter
(To Mdhara Kabvakacha on Heroes' Day)

he wanted his voice to assume the madness of the gun,
to tell his nonchalant audience
that those five years in the bush were not spent for fun
but here, in this ambience
of Dube's bar in Ruya,
the gun refused to be conjured up
and remained trapped in a world outside Ruya,
outside our thoughts of good after-beer fucks.

he wanted his voice to assume fear's disposition,
to wear that dreaded skeletal garment
that filled his heart with trepidation
and assumed the colours of apparel worn for an eerie sacrament,
but our numb minds,
made number by Dube's intoxicants,
kept the fear at bay even though it tried
to slither in like Eve's serpent.

he wanted his voice to assume the revolutionary hate
that he said drove him into the forest
to help create this bittersweet fate
that has given us no rest,
but his visceral hatred of what is gone
failed to recreate itself in our hearts
because we only knew these ruins of Stone
and the coals on top of which we placed our butts.

he wanted to sing us a song
about Nehanda and Kaguvi and Chitepo,

a song about the mighty and strong
on whose graves grew flowers with the colour purple,
but our blind eyes could not see phantoms,
they could only see a tyrant
who ruthlessly fed us on maggots
with the garrulous arrogance of a pirate.

slowly his eyes glazed
with the watery film of lost hope
for the bornfree's minds were a maze
in whose labyrinths the torch of revolution had not shone,
so he stared into space,
into the forest that appeared before his eyes,
and he saw a time and place
when he mattered as a cadre in that fight.

freedom
(To Freedom Nyamubaya and Chenjerai Hove)

Freedom's shadow disappears around a corner
leaving behind an apparition for sad eyes to gaze at
through the slits of a suffocating existence.

time is frozen in this facility built by political sadists
to murder the spirits of those who hope,
who want a flame of love to burn in their hearts.

where freedom used to throne herself like a goddess
a yawning hole stares skywards like an accusation
while a blind moon stares back and shrugs hunched shoulders.

these ruins
(To Nicholas 'Dzimbahwerichazovei' Nyachega)

ruin
ruin ruins
ruin ruins ruining
ruin ruins ruining ruined
ruin ruins ruining ruined ruinous
ruin ruins ruining ruined ruinous ruination

is it just me
or the ruins just keep expanding?

on these ruins
(written 2km from Zuva Service Station, Belgravia, Harare, 8/1/19)

the elders want these ruins to be sparkling clean
because on these ruins
the anus could not resist
the purging power of shit
landing softly on the upturned face
of one of the ancestors.

the elders want these ruins to be sparkling clean
because some libidinous revellers
could not resist the urge
to thrust away their rage
astride splayed and shrivelled thighs
while the gods gawked at them with envy.

the elders want these ruins to be sparkling clean
because the revellers could not resist
the soothing exit of urine
from their extended and erect phalluses
onto the sun-baked backs
of the rocks that make the ruins.

now the elders want to speak to Stone
but Stone does not hear them
because Stone's desecration
has closed the path to the ancestors
and only when the ruins become sparkling clean
can the path be opened again.

but even as the old women gather the firewood

for the opaque brew of the ancestors
the shitter is contorting his face
astride the silent ruins,
the piss of the reveller
continues to commit sacrilege
on the bold heads of the rocks
and the fucker now fucks
with the rage of thirty seven years
and two more
of elusive orgasms.

leaving
(to the emigrant)

sometimes leaving is not easy,
it's different from when the baby cries all night
and you pick a stray blanket and pillow
to find a space for your tired body on the couch.

with this kind of leaving
you have to un-cremate memories,
make them live and tag along with you,
make them lug the landscapes that make them real
to paste them on the tarmacs of newfoundland.

some things are easier said than done;
our mouths leave when they speak about leaving
yet we remain rooted to the same spaces
fearing to brave the rootlessness of wandering,
but one day, when you finally close your mouth
know that you have slammed the door
and that it's time you took your things and left.

some truths about people and about countries
are arrived at coincidentally
without seeming to do so.

insanity

sometimes I don't know who to hunt
whose body to press against the wall and plant
saliva-moistened lips to supple ones
and congratulate myself when the deed is done.

sometimes I don't know what to write
which intoxicated words to invite
to a poetry summit that will end
with words lying carelessly on paper, spent.

sometimes I don't know whether this world
 should explode into fragments or just fold
into a messy heap like a mad man's blanket
after a night of shagging the phantoms of this planet.

sometimes I don't know whether to pray for rain
or let the heat spank this stoic plain,
let it squirm and turn at least
as a sign that at last it too is pissed.

sometimes I don't know how to attempt
anything that does not complete
a cycle that can easily be interpreted
as insanity on steroids
eating a man's brain away,
itself an interpretation that can sway
the faith of those who want to take me seriously.

madness

1

the tired grin of a diarrhoea-oozing anus
the desperate smile of the bread at the famished cockroach
the gluttonous embrace of the emperor's teeth
the hasty retreat of a desiccated phallus
the arrogance of flared nostrils stealing our air
because —

the king and the dog were close friends
then the king ate the dog.

I must not tire of telling this lie
until it becomes a truth.

the sun and the moon once embarked on a conjugal journey
during which the rays of the sun pierced into the woman and the hare
graffited in the womb of the moon,
the orgasm ripped them out of the moon
and now the woman and the hare live in my head.

there was once a man who decided to challenge Lightning to a fight
when Lightning's relatives who had come to watch saw the man
they cried and embraced him
and called him Thunder.

someone touched the hem of my smile
the fart ripped the country apart
because power is thicker than blood
look! see those trees? right there!
their ears have been hacked off by overzealous disciples
there is a yawning hole in the head of the master.

flowers have small tits
from which bees suckle.

2

the clip clap of fading footsteps in the corridor
the groan of thunder receding into the mountains
the tired shamble of a lion that has hunted in vain
the thoughtful growl of an empty stomach –
one day peace decided to have children –

the mangy dog also fought to mount the steamy bitch
he scratched,
he raved,
he barked,
he took murderous bites,
he pranced about like a berserk phallus
then collapsed before the entrance of the bitch's vagina
dead.

the putrid smell of the entrails of the dog
that Dickie roasted for gullible revellers
the sluggish flow of the Ndenda River
the sighs of the wind groping in the darkness of the forest
the deafening pride of a famous cuckold
the dirt underwear worn by the grass on the anthill
the soldier, the woman and the crocodile
the woman
the soldier and the crocodile
one of them is alone.

there is a house in my head
with forlorn eyes for windows.

3

the Chamavara and the Chiriga mountains
sitting majestically on that plain like the breasts of a spirit medium
the laboured crow of the old cock
the farmer gazing desperately at the plain sky.

there is a house in my head
and a cemetery wherein lie living people
and voices that are hushed into whispers by the wind
the soldier, the child and the crocodile
the child
the soldier and the crocodile
one of them is alone.

one day a group of people gathered
to bring down a tower using their voices
they cried
they shouted
they howled
they sang
they prayed
when they stopped, the tower had grown taller
then they went back home nursing dry throats.

a e i o u
mha mhe mhi mho mhu
mhara mhere mhiri mhoro mhuru
mba mbe mbi mbo mbu
mbara mbere mbiri...

two flies are kissing while perched on the horn of a teapot
beside the teapot is the map of a country.

4

the sword refused to be demoted to a ploughshare
and ravaged the land of the people who dared demote it,
ravaged and ravaged and left streams of blood
to water the peace of the sword.

the earth writhing under the rays of the witching sun
the river roaring, spinning and tearing its clothes
before falling asleep in the restless ocean's embrace
therein lies the paradox —

peace has a name
sadness has a name
the rumble in my stomach has a name
the echoes in the mountains speak of a war
that too has a name.

what is your name? asked the frog
isn't it obvious? replied Obvious.

the birth of a cockroach is a nonchalant one
the bullet and the beast laugh death over a beer
where they are joined by bayonet the joker
and the three plan their after-beer fucks
beast, bullet, bayonet, beer.

I am a veteran of this life
I have clawed and scraped,
I have screwed and screamed,
I have pushed and pulled,
and even after all this
they want to keep the nigger boy running
let's talk about rights —

whales
sharks
snakes
ants
flies
Cecil the lion

5

the bemused look on the face of the evening star
the sideway glance of a libidinous cock
the perfect connection of a female donkey's twofold kick
against the inclined neck of the horny male
the tired voice of a chicken stealthily entering a fowl run
some kinds of existence…

I drown in the crowd of my thoughts
and try to catch a single one
to scrutinise it and understand its anatomy
but all of them slip through the slimy fingers of my mind
so I give up and fart on them
to drown myself in the gratuitous pleasure of having the last laugh.

one day the dogs of a compound decided to commit a crime
they ransacked the kitchen hut,
they turned the pots upside down,
they fought for the pieces of dry meat hanging above the fireplace,
and when the owners of the compound came back
they slaughtered the chickens for the crimes of the dogs.

let revelation come
and unveil the cadaver of the ignorance that lords over us.

6

the swish-swish of grazing cattle
the damp smell of upturned soil
the shy smile of the peeping sun
the strained conversation between father and son
the creaking of an ox-drawn cart going uphill
the cowardly darkness coming at the heels of the setting sun.

I am the unwanted fart that comes during an anthem
I am the darkness of a dream that haunts the head of the sleeper
I am the rat that gnaws at the bread of the children
I am the mischievous cloud that holds the winter sun in its dark
palm.

the riotous din in the rats' parliament
the soporific smile of sunlight in the eyes of a drunkard
the sustained moan of a dying cow
the tottering steps of a tired storm.

the smile came but it had missing teeth
so they decided to buy it new ones
after three days they found the smile dead by the roadside
with a gap where the new teeth used to be.

each man struts around with a pit for a shadow
that pit has a name
strut strut strut strut strut
until, tired, he lays himself to sleep in his shadow.

the storm came and went
but not without promising to come back again.

7

the streets were empty when I went to school in the morning
when I came back in the evening they were crowded
with people and things,
with voices,
with desperation distending from a thousand faces
                    a thousand and one apparitions.

between life and death,
between going to school and coming back,
the distance is the same
a lot happens in-between
but the first one gives you the impression of time running berserk,
unhinged time
time ganging up with mortality
to laugh at those who spend their time trying to forget.

the glass that sits before me has splayed its legs
for my imperious and elaborate entrance;
it writhes maniacally under me
and I thrust and thrust as if that's the only thing that matters;
when the deed is finally done
my feet stammer their way home.

there was a high level of procedure to the madness
until those who were sane also decided to become mad.

8

the scarred history that lords over me
the bullet riddled lie that cannot look me in the eye
the charred remains of an all along elusive future

the piercing shrill of a bloodthirsty mosquito.

there is a country whose citizens' eyes are crimson balls of fire,
bloodshot irises that look like optical wounds;
they have been gazing too long at a dream
until the dream vomited blood into their eyes.

one day Hope and Gloom had an altercation,
they had picked my head on their way from the pub
and each was claiming ownership of it;
my head looked at them and shouted,
"Get thee behind me motherfuckers!"
Hope sped off in one direction,
Gloom in another
and my head slept for ages after that.

 the wounds of the sky
sparkle in the darkness of the night.

9

(sigh)
to write…
to write is to gather the world into a bundle
that I can walk with,
that I can walk on,
that I can walk towards,
that I can exorcise out of myself.

to write is to sanctify this madness
that runs amok in my head,
to give it meaning,
to divest it of meaning,
to cry,

to smile,
to laugh uproariously
while shaking hands with the phantoms of my existence.

a bleak derision lords over our lives.

one day I met the moon looking for the hare and the woman
her heart was bleeding from the wounds of conjugal lacerations.

the hare and the woman have made a fire in my head
and my ears are breathing out the smoke of it.

10

the arrogance of repetition which we force into a variety of costumes
blue
yellow
orange
white
black
red
green
purple
pink
brown
one actor painting himself into several characters for a duplicitous
audience.
#Life#Madness#UselessWords#RamblingsOfAGhettoIdiot#Becaus
eSadnessIsBeautiful

it is only in squatting astride the yawning hole of the pit latrine
that the emperor and his subjects share pieces of democracy

the midnight preacher
(Zimbabwe, 13 January 2019)

the apostles who flanked him
looked glum, as if this was the last supper
but it wasn't, at least according to him
because he would come back for his flock
which he would in the meantime
leave in the hands of the apostles.

then after a rambling sermon,
during which we listened with our eyes,
he cursed his flock
and left the apostles as executors of the curse.

open defecation

from the breasts of our mothers
we learnt that to shit
is a very private affair
but we cannot help but gaze up
at the anus of the emperor
when he chooses to undress
for the voyeurs underneath.

we stare at the hairy buttocks
and open our mouths in wonder
while asking ourselves,
what kind of ancestral fortune
has bequeathed so much hair
on the buttocks of a mere mortal?

we laugh at the peristaltic
contraction of the wrinkles
of the scarlet anus of the emperor
and marvel at the ugliness of it
while asking ourselves,
if the anus is this ugly thing
what about the mouth?

we gaze up at the bizarre contractions
and try to match anus and mouth.
we open our mouths in wonder,
we open our mouths to laugh,
but wonder and laughter
suffer stillbirths
because the gaping mouths
provide cavernous repositories

for the shit that shoots out
from the wrinkled folds
of the emperor's anus.

the benefits of hygiene

he showed up in my hood
dressed like a man whose sole purpose
was to preach the benefits of hygiene

> hygiene
> / hayijini /

> Noun

> A condition promoting sanitary practices.

I am not sure about the condition part
but from the way he spoke
there was hygiene everywhere except here
where mucus-stained faces peered through broken glass,
where rivers tumbled into the confinement
of various assortments of waste.

his white coat looked like an exhibit
of how we were supposed to live our lives
without soiling them with the desperation
that drifted with the dust to settle
in the crevices of flared nostrils,
flared to catch meagre wafts of air
before the contamination that vibrated from our lives
had sucked every particle to oblivion.

I watched him closely
although I could not see his mouth and nose
which were covered to ward off
the daily grains of our existence

that floated in the air around him
together with the sighs of our skins
that gave a putrid character to the air around us.

I watched him and marvelled at how possible it was
to achieve this hygiene he was talking about:
wear a white coat
cover your mouth and nose
stop sniffing
stop feeling
stop hearing
just talk
talk
talk until the dust-clogged ears of your audience
become complicit in these hallucinations of hygiene,
until the dusty butts of your audience
begin to enjoy the head's dream
of supple comforts that will come in the future.

the revenge of the oppressed

the emperor's hilarious misstep
(sanitised as 'breaking the fall'),
or his nodding visage
as he dozes before his subordinates
(sanitised as 'listening'),

the emperor's emaciated epidermis
dotted with haphazard patterns of ailing,
or his writhing in the merciless hands of heat
while muttering and contorting his face
like a child giving birth to a country,

the emperor's tongue committing heinous crimes
against the sacrosanct English of Her Majesty
and that of the silent ancestors,
the emperor's tongue fumbling and fumbling
and bringing linguistic traffic to a jam,

the emperor soiling his pants,
or failing to find a way with his flaccid implement
which consigns him to the world of eternal cuckolds,

these ephemeral moments,
these moments when the emperor struts around naked
are the moments when he hangs on a spike
in the heads of the oppressed

Some things happen in the head

portrait of the poet as a middle-aged man

many metaphors are quarrelling
and causing an uproar in my mind;
I am not tipsy; I am only sieving
through the clutter in my mind
which makes me forget my body sometimes
and disremember the fact that the feet of the mind
are occasionally a million light years away
from the uncertain ones that plod the dusty paths of this life.

there is a straggly thought that is crawling
to infinite spaces whereon are sprawling
many things that I should have done...
read a book, tilled a garden, gnawed at a bone
while contemplating life's anatomy,
its entrails, the things that I can fathom.

regret has painted the walls of my mind
 with the hurried graffiti of an impudent youth:
I should have pressed her body against mine!
I should have taken my time to savour the smoothness of her skin!
I should have allowed my tongue to unlock her erotic bounty!
I should have...!

I shouldn't have hesitated!
I shouldn't have vacillated!
I shouldn't have shilly-shallied!
I shouldn't have...

so many things to do
yet so little time left!!

what if…
(dark thoughts)

what if the missing teeth of the moon
are the reason why I can't chew this bone?

what if these silent journeys
are harbingers of silence's eternal reign?

what if this incarcerated smile
morphs into a guttural cry?

what if beyond the cliff edge of this moment
I fall into all the happiness the world can offer?

what if these two are not one
but many fleshy layers crying for air?

what if these words are just fugitives
scuttling away from the recognition of the reader?

forgetting

the line breaks somewhere.
these haphazard (dis)connections give a sense
of reality running berserk,
of unhinged constituents sliding away
from the regime of memory.

time is this thick mist.
the echoes of lost travellers' desperate calls
fumble through the unforgiving mist
to be absorbed into the rocky embraces
of prankster landscapes.

history is a mad cacophony of voices.
they fly in the wind like crazy insects
buzzing and buzzing and causing a din
that bids you to stick fingers in your ears
or yell at the motherfuckers to stop or you'll shoot.

I'll shoot at phantoms.
I'll shoot at voices.
I'll shoot at history.
I will shoot at the mist.
I will shoot...

I will shoot until the smoke
and the bratatat of the gun
obliterate certain things from my memory.
reflections

how did I get here?
which mischievous hand directed me here?
how did all my archived fear

end up being fulfilled this way?

when did this space shrink to this size?
when did I start wanting to make a huge stride
only to end up stepping on the edges
like a story suffocated
by the claustrophobics of pages?

which sign did my heart bid me to follow
that I now in this despicable uncertainty wallow?
why are promises so treacherous
that my trust in them has made life so perilous?

I reflect and let out innumerable sighs
and tell myself that I won't trust signs
for signs are like the weather,
entertaining caprices at the slightest turn of a feather.

roots

as I sink these roots deep into this soil
I fear that some overzealous hooligan
will come and dig.

the things I do

I want to stare at the rays of the sun,
to open my pupils and say, sun where is your blinding sting?
to hold those rays with my eyebrows for fun,
to have them caress my face and cling
to the supple softness of it.

I want to stare at the half moon at night,
to stare and wonder where the other half went,
what sort of reckless and insatiable might
stole half of the moon and sent
the other half to float miserably like a left-over reject
across that star-speckled slate?

I want to stare at the river,
at the soft caresses it gives to frogs and crabs
and get mad with the jealous
of a jilted lover who is nursing stabs
from hands that are callous
and do not know how to love.

I want to stare at the horizon,
at the point where the mountain touches the sky,
where blue lips kiss the rocky dome
and suckle it until it runs dry;
I want to stare, and touch
with eyes that have seen how peace is longed for in the heart.

I want to stare at the bees
suckling a flower's tit
and wish I could squeeze
the fecund bulge on which

the tit gracefully rests
without squeezing life out of it.

the things I do
are done only when I wish.

pauses between my pride

my blackness is a song
that lifts its feet for a dance.

the children want their bread
but someone has defecated in the tray.

my blackness is nature's affirmation
of my eternal union with it.

angry cyclones have come
and carried away a generation.

my blackness is beauty
wearing the body of a mortal.

something is decimating my body
at a time when the cost of dying has gone up.

stains

what do you do
with stains that dare obliterate the beauty of the stars?
with stains that stain the flag of your memory?
with stains that stain the whites of the eye?
with stains that stain the history that hides in silence?
with stains that frequently drop onto your shrinking space?
and when you try to clean up the mess
and you find out that you are leaving your own mess
in the wake of your meticulous scrubbing...
what do you do?

stains stain my memory
stains stain my history
stains stain my flag
stains stain the whites of my eyes
stains stain my space.

I am a child of stains
and I too am a stain
staying here to be stained
and stain in my own way
the stained life that I live!

on finding yourself with nothing to do

sometimes you find yourself with nothing to do
like a storm after surveying its messy handiwork
and asking itself what the fuck the noise was all about
I mean, after all this hysterical anger, what else?

the WI-FI connection here has sanctions,
the girl who has many layers of powder
quarrelling for attention on her face
matter-of-factly informs you
that the password is for those who have bought something;
you haven't, because there is nothing to buy
and the empty shelves flaunt themselves at you
like retired prostitutes who still think they got a thing.

your first thought is to pen a poem about the vast emptiness
shrouding the land like the silence of a cemetery
but you're fucking tired of sad poems
or angry poems in which syllables hurtle towards a precipice.
when you have nothing to do
the next thing you do must jolt you
to walk around looking for a good fuck,
or a cigarette, or a beer,
or weed.

fuck! Some motherfucker is playing mischief with events,
every incident is reluctant to happen
as if it needs something to give it a dose of motivation
you know, like what you do with the poker face
at the passport office
who tells you nonchalantly, sorry no passport paper
and you take out some greens that you wave like some conjurer

68

making the paper appear, crisp and fresh
as if it has disembarked from the morning flight.

morning runs into afternoon
and when afternoon and night collide
it requires monumental exertion
for you to tell which is which,
so you curse and stare at the gathering darkness
without seeing it,
without wanting to see it,
because not seeing is in itself an event.

some ruminations take place
while you are sitting on a bar stool;
some confessions are made
after the searing flow of booze
down your oesophagus.

bar stool ruminations

there are paradisiac pleasures hiding in that skirt;
all I need is a liquor-assisted momentary flirt
or a wobbly dance that will persuade
the skirt to travel up on its own and extenuate
freewill.

we need a reason tomorrow, don't we?
beer and dance have always been reliable, haven't they?
when trouser zippers go astray
we slur, "Sorry, this zip is failing to stay,
should be the beer, or some mischievous play
it's not a big deal, no?"

and when she says it's no big deal
I surrender myself into the arms of the dream
and let feverish desire's beam
light the way into the night's secrets.

"Ah! Secrets!" remarks a man who disturbs my reverie
"For the likes of us there are two secrets:
Secrets ensconced in the folds of the night
and secrets sandwiched between seductive thighs."

2 keys
(Zimbabwe, after the price of beer had gone up)

sometimes the only key you need
is this searing agony peristalting
down your unsuspecting oesophagus;
but even this too is a lost key,
a lost cause.

drunk talk

my neighbour's wife is a beautiful lady;
I hope she thinks the same about her neighbour's husband
because the fantasies I play in my head
require a certain level of reciprocity.

come on man, you perish such fantasies!
another man's wife is trouble;
picture a crocodile:
now let's suppose, for the sake of supposing
that the crocodile has a wife,
would you go for her?

hell no man!

now, that's how it should be with another man's wife.

but he is no crocodile, man!
besides, he's been gone,
gone like last month's moon.
ok, forget the moon bit,
but he's been gone like forever
and I can see the arms of her eyes
directing me to the bulging suppleness
that sits on her bosom
like twin islands on a sea of pleasure,
what do you expect me to do with that?

well, the crocodile part didn't work.
ok, think of invading the president's palace
and ordering him to surrender the country to you
because you have a better plan for it,
would you do that shit?

hell man, we did that!
remember that time when we played around with those tanks
like kids savouring lunar park fantasies?
I can do that shit man.

damn! Nothing is working here!
hey girl! Do you have a concoction
to pacify the hormones of this poor fellow
whose death wish is written in garish colours
like a politician's banner flying aloft
a sea of uncultured garbage?

he needs a woman like me,
someone whose dexterity will annihilate
the unbridled cravings in his loins
that make him fancy an absent neighbour's wife.

show him! Show him what you have girl!
let this demon be exorcised from his loins!
let him be set free from this death wish!
let what heaven concealed behind that dress
open the eyes of this man
that he may see the pleasures that reside
away from the supple body of his neighbour's wife.

come on guys! this is the twenty-first century
the only thing to fear
is the world running berserk
because some trigger-happy western kids
are in the habit of playing hooky
using some technologies that feed on human limbs.

fuck it man! You are irredeemable

but that should not stop you
from decorating this table
with the divine experiment of Charles Glass,
or were you playing hooky when you promised
like those western kids whose people voted presidents?

remembering is sweet and hilarious
when you move your tongue
along the right edges.

Gwayagwaya Braai Stand
(To Tawanda Chambwe)

one evening, Dickie sold us salty biltong
at Gwayagwaya & Sons Bottle Store.
at midnight, while drunk from song,
none noticed the absence of the deaf dog
who loved to sleep all night long
on the bottle store's old floor.

Chaucer's pie chart
(to Philani Amadeus Nyoni)

after a colossal attempt to torture us with Pythagoras
during which we asked one question
then two
then three
then four

the teacher ranted:
you are dunderheads!
your fathers are dunderheads!
your mothers are dunderheads!
all your people are dunderheads!

we remained silent
and waited for the whole charade to end...

then Chaucer came

he had spent the whole morning
conversing with phantoms at the township dumpsite.

he usurped the chalk from the teacher
and drew a pie chart on the chalkboard.

with bloodshot, eyes he looked at us
and gruffly said,
"Everything is on the pie chart,"
before bolting out.

suddenly, we all saw the way to Damascus.

where I come from
(Masvingo, Zimbabwe)

the smell of upturned soil is fecund with life,
the crickets' chorus is a song to the gods,
the low and thoughtful growl in the sky
and the skeletal lights that write themselves
from east to west on the laden sky's dark base
are the harbingers of the gods' tears
pelting the scorched earth to give it life.

the children running in shirttails are not naked;
they want the rainy embraces of the gods
to clothe their skins in watery apparel,
and in turn the gods will receive from the children
the greatest gift of all:
the laughter of the children hurtling
across the undulating plains of the savannah.

the cattle running and kicking the air with their hind legs
and mock fighting phantoms with their horns
are not running away from the herd boys;
they are merely running to the stream
to assuage their thirst after a good day at the pastures.
the calves are running ahead with vigour
because life is this vast expanse before them,
but the elderly ones, who have seen it all,
are running thoughtfully, with the contentment of old age.

the axe that grandfather is brandishing at grandmother
is not meant to slice her into two;
grandfather and grandmother are merely dancing

to the accompaniment of the drum.
grandmother is dancing with cultured grace
while grandfather is flapping his grey-white dustcoat.
they are both wearing crisscrossing tyre sandals
which are receiving every ounce of sound
from the hide-strapped seed shakers around their legs.

Blocks 1-13, Magamba Hostels

Block 1
there is a face staring down at the bustle of Siyaso,
staring through one of the unblinking eyes
of the last floor that looks like the neighbour of the skies.
when you stare up at the face from the dust of Siyaso,
you feel the reverence that clothes the prayers of the saints
whose faces are turned up to accompany the incense
that they send up as words seasoned with songs.

Block 2
they said Mbalo was squashed to a stain
at the zebra crossing that leads to Mupedzanhamo,
so they mourn him with songs and beer
and the voice of Maria which vanquishes the air around her,
and the swivelling buttocks of Winnet
which provide fodder for those who can conjure
images of themselves astride those buttocks
on a cold winter night.

Block 3
the God's Embassy preacher is on fire;
he is saying that sinners will burn in a pit
and that Magamba Hostels has supplied quite a handful.
he stands alone in the dust with his bible
while the sinners go about their business
of selling weed and smoking it and smoking it again
and trying to get a glimpse of their receding consciousness.

Block 4
the party chairman is addressing a crowd of women;

81

he is saying we can never be a colony again,
he is saying our sovereignty is precious,
he is saying the supreme leader came from God.
the women ululate and break into a song
about bones that rose and wore the body of a man
to return the country to its rightful owners.

Block 5
the youth are dancing to a song about birds,
about birds that hop from here to there,
about birds that can be raised before our faces
to send the reflection of our faces back to us,
birds that do not chop tomatoes with their beaks,
birds that can be shared all around
until every youth in Magamba owns one.

Block 6
old man Gaza's daily 6 o'clock rant is going on;
his words are a sword that cuts to the staple of power
until bloodied limbs of authority and its people lie at his feet
like victims of that legendary moment of madness
that turned the waters of the river into blood.
he rants and rants and rants, old man Gaza
until, tired, he shambles into the hostel to rant another day.

Block 7
two people are engaged in the business of clawing each other
for reasons that are consumed by the fight;
they claw each other until their clothes, afraid, take flight
and leave sweaty bodies locked in battle
while the voyeurs lick their lips and swallow hard.
they fight for eternity until eternity slinks away,
and with it the crowd of voyeurs who love things that end.

Block 8
Pablo the barber loves to display and sell heads;
he has heads pasted on a glossy poster:
round heads, pickaxe heads, haulage truck heads
small boys heads, grown up men heads.
people come to Pablo and, for some coins, ask him
to interpret the poster heads on their own dishevelled heads
after which they will walk with the whole world in their heads.

Block 9
"our tower light is brighter than that of block 13!"
"our toilets are cleaner than those of block 6!"
"our girls are more beautiful than all the Magamba girls!"
"Shogo is a better thief than Ghetto!"
"our president is more popular than Trump!"
"Messi plays better than Ronaldo!"
"watch your mouth motherfucker!"

Block 10
the children are playing in the rain;
they are scooping handfuls of puddle
and flinging them at each other's faces
until they look like apparitions of the undead.
the mothers are watching through the windows
and rehearsing how they will smack those buttocks
while reminding the children that soap is not stone.

Block 11
there is a boy who is dipping his stick into a tin of ink
and drawing people's visages on the wall.
his excellency's face is quarrelling for space
with the face of a toddler who is holding ganga
while pouting out rings of smoke from his mouth.
"united we stand divided we fall!"

"forward ever backward never!"

Block 12
there is a group of people holding hoses;
they are fighting a stream of shit
that is distending from where the shitfall hits the ground.
the watery assault is too much for the shit
and like a tired snake it slithers away
accompanied by a victory chorus from the shitfighters
who pat each other on the back for a victory well-earned.

block 13
the boys are kicking around a plastic ball
and wearing jerseys with names on scribbled their backs:
Ronaldo
Messi
Mane
Neymar
Salah.
their dreams are in the plastic ball,
a bundle that they kick around
to the delight of the watchers.

then love came
and I became...
sad
happy
sad
happy
sa...
ha...

emptying

hunger's foreman has swept clean my insides
and gathered the debris near the exit;
the cavernous pit latrine waits in anticipation
as I squat astride its yawning hole.

my thoughts are like desperate passengers
trying to catch the last bus home;
they are scratching the walls of my mind,
scratching
pushing
howling
squeezing
farting
and only a disinterested verse police
can restore sanity and force
the thoughts to respect the traffic rules of words.

my heart is brimming with passions untold
and sometimes I drown in the sea that they are.
I need a saviour to release the waters
and ride with me on their riotous flow
to be deposited where the sand and the sun kiss,
a paradise of passion and romance.

winter poem
(a bachelor's song)

there are many kinds of love
but when winter comes, I feel all of them.

losing

I do not know why things happen like this:
that I rehearse every line meticulously,
scrutinise each one for those weak spots
that might make hard-earned words tumble out
before they reach their intended destination.

yet when the time to utter them comes
this stammer that comes like an unwanted fart
tears apart the carefully made lines
unclothing them of all feeling
so that words remain inside
to leave me a prisoner of the unsaid.

to a love unreciprocated

we were two travellers traversing landscapes
that crisscrossed so much that we met severally
and I made a footnote in my heart
that if there was some going back
it would be to those points that made us meet;
I made the footnote in the hope that you did too
because love is when hearts speak in whispers
that tumble out to stand at the edge of sound.

but even as the landscapes crisscrossed
the whispers of our hearts didn't,
and so my heart's whisper stands on the edge of sound
staring across this vastness with no whisper in sight
except the sighs of this lonely, tired wind
which has traversed so many landscapes
that it has forgotten
what it feels like to be still and be loved.

stranger

I want to write a poem about her,
about how the one who sculptured her
bridged the gap between poetry and divinity,
but words have mutinied against
the intensity of electrified passion
and only a few unadventurous ones
have lined up before me to capture
a June afternoon's pleasant surprise to solitude's companion,
leaving me with no option except to think about

how, when she appeared
in the pale sunlight of June,
my eyes pierced and tore to threads
the veil of loneliness that had murdered my shadow;
how, when she appeared,
she became a home to wandering passions,
opening her Noah's Ark wide
for fortunate emotions to file in...
saved at last.

Post-verse: So when I came back during a dark night to confirm
what I thought had happened inside, she waited for me by the gate,
and the car's beam seemed to pay homage to her enigmatic
silhouette, ensconced in a nightgown that hid, and revealed at the
same time, the mysteries of creation at night.

falling

when I gazed down at her
she looked like a vast vista
that you look down upon from the summit of a mountain,
you know, that kind that makes you want to fall
and be hugged by the misty blueness of it,
but falling is not something you do on a whim;
in nightmares it feels like the shattering of your limbs,
an elongated postponement of contact
that makes you want to scream against the waiting,
against the sadistic suspension of closure.

what if the falling takes the form of a nightmare,
a nightmare in which darkness and light quarrel,
in which your voice hysterically struggles,
poking tiny fists at the unforgiving walls of your throat
and, giving up, collapsing back into the abyss of your being?

she came

when she came, she became the cumulative gathering
of all the passions of childhood and youth,
the overflow of all the waters of emotion
that I had dammed to stop the river
from carrying me to the unknown.

when she came, she became the rhyme
that made words pick beautiful steps:
a spring,
a swivelling of the parts that mattered
to the gratuitous delight of the gazing eye.

when she came, she became the flesh
that for long periods had hidden in words
which had hidden in song
which had hidden in sounds
whose patterns had hidden from the fingers
that had sought to trace them.

when she came, she became.

kiss
(to Villes Seti Chidora)

before falling into your arms that afternoon,
that afternoon when there was no trouble in sight,
I always thought of a kiss
as the tongue of the moon
savouring the watery skin of the sea at night,
or a covetous flower swivelling to the angle of the sun
to receive the touch of sunlight's lips on its expectant ones,
or timid raindrops before the beginning of a storm
tapping the bold dome of a mountain
to provide respite from the thermal assault of the sun.

but now that I have kissed you
I think a kiss is a heart
basking in the bounteous promises
of what it means to keep someone prisoner
in that corner of the heart that has for long
defied the lure of hungry eyes and seductive smiles.

we danced

here is where we danced,
in the dust,
around the smouldering fire
that looked like mischief
engaged in a hair-raising duel
with the opaque darkness.

you held my hand
and led me around the fire
in a tribal way
like it was some initiation ritual
or the yearly dance of maidens and men
except that here, it was just us:
                    you and me
                    and the dark sky above.

here is where we stopped,
                    suddenly!
to listen to our beating hearts
that whispered feverishly to each other
in words undecipherable to our dawdling minds
but which nonetheless spoke to limbs and lips
until limbs and lips moved
in unison
                              a chorus
                              an upswing
                              a mad crescendo!

then an epiphany
and the denouement of tired bodies

locked in the aftermath of amorous combat
that had no voyeurs
except the fire
and the stars
blinking from the base of the dark sky above.

this is where we sat
while the watery tongue of the river
lapped at our suspended ankles
with the eagerness of our lips and limbs,
and you giggled like a mermaid
except that I had never seen a mermaid before
until that day at the edge of the river
when you giggled
at the watery kiss of the river.

you remember this jugged mass of rocks right?
how the rocks huddled together
and looked like the bizarre castle of mischievous gods?
do you remember the selfie stick
how, when you lifted it,
you looked like a goddess,
an enchanting water goddess chanting an incantation?
that did it!
the hypnotic spell claimed its victims
and the rocks witnessed a desecration of the castle
by two mortal souls
who, for a short while, looked like gods.

you remember this footpath right?
how it snaked through the grass
like a mystery trail in a game of hidden treasures
except that the treasures were not hidden there
but in us,

in the bodies that gyrated towards each other
with the surreal grace of dancing friendly witches.

the path led to a nest
and the nest is memory
because memory and grass are friends
I keep forgetting the poet who said these words
but since I live my life on memories
I remember us,
I remember the path that led to the nest,
I remember the nest,
and I remember the gyrating bodies
that unlocked virgin bounty
for consummation by two mortal souls
that were you and me.

we sat here on this ledge remember?
and watched the golden ball of fire
as it glided towards western secrets,
but the west was no secret,
the secret was in the whispers of the wind
and the whispers of two hearts,
hearts whose embrace was made divine
by the halo of the one eyed horizon.

my heart said:
there is a garden in which mortals commit no sin,
to that garden let us hasten
and stay together to tire the serpent
who comes when we are apart.

your heart said:
I revel in our nakedness
in the glow of our skins in the afternoon sun

and the tug that brings bodies together
ensconcing them in an amorous halo
that blinds envious spinster gods.

so we went to the garden;
the garden was you
the garden was me.

the moon and you

for the first time, the new moon is full
a miracle!
the stars have slinked away in reverence,
nature has said, not unto us
but to love be the honour.
so it's just the moon and you
and a man caught between light and love.

to be loved

eyes can sing a song
that only the heart can hear,
lips can hug the mind
in ways the tongue can't explain.

about last night

she looked at me matter-of-factly
and told me that last night did not go as planned,
that it took heaven and earth to coax me
to surrender my body and mind
to the sweetness of two mortals' union.

I mumbled something about purgation,
"From the word 'purge,' you know honey?"
but looking back, I don't know what the hell it was all about.

purge? purgation? purgatory?
does it really matter?

heartbreak

I look at her and don't know how to say
it was a momentary flirt meant for mere play
and that my heart's door remained closed;
for how can a heart that she owns be cloned?
how can anything compare
to the eyes that make my heart flare
with fiery passions that light the future,
a future that I will spend with a soul so pure?

balanced life

I fell because I loved
I rose because I loved
I fell...
I...

growing old can be such a bore

life

she led me to the house at the end of the street
and left her caresses on my face.

Papa said
(to a young man)

the day you were born was your morn,
time travel will take you to your eve
the one to whom you will cling
and the one through whom you will exit,
but while it lasts, love, laugh, smile, cry
because life is our way of doing such.

innocence
(to Abigirl Katsande)

innocence is on that face
that smiles together with the eyes,
a face that is like sunlight
perforating the dark clouds of existence
to give to life a golden hue.

but wait until villainous moments
gang up and seize the face to fix on it
a bizarre network of furrows –
life's handiwork banishing innocence
to idle reminiscences.

nature too has those moments
when it is not angry
and only wants to give us,
though short-lived, moments of bliss

sunset

sunset is the knowing wink of the sinking sun,
the hallowed kiss of this eternal lover
on a face upturned in amorous anticipation,
the gentle caress of a golden hand
on bosoms that hunger for love.

sunset is the lazy eye that gazes
at a receding and laidback village
whose huts hug the foot of a mountain
like ancestral beads on the leg of a maiden
before the yearly rain dance.

sunset is the farewell embrace of a lover
whose departure is fecund with promises
of a return that will be heralded by another halo
and a chorus sung by voices that speak no malice,
untroubled hearts that harbour no vice.

Chigovanyika sunset

voices create a forest in which intelligibility loses its way
and, giving up, it mingles with the dust
and the golden hue of the sinking sun
that for an infinitesimal moment
hallows the walls inebriated by age
into surreal brooding figurines.

some nostalgias are sweet
others are not;
but nostalgia is just like that.

nostalgia

those nomads fed themselves on a diet of manna,
that magical crust that clothed the desert floor every morning,
until they started to hallucinate about Pharaoh,
that benevolent and majestic king,
who became an incarnation of how life was to be lived
away from the drudgery of the wilderness and Moses.

shit smells nicer
when you flare your nostrils to draw in air
from what should be a pungent pool of history
but which now feels
like a repository of all the happiness allocated to you
by whoever is responsible for allocating happiness
to the beings that strut around on this earth,
including yourself.

past rivers flowed with the grace of Eden before the fall
past food tasted like thoughts of sex before the first time
and your faith was like a mountain
moving mustard seeds around like toys;
and Christmas!
it tasted pristinely fresh back then
as if the baby who was born in the manger
was still contemplating which voice to use
to announce to the world that he was here!

Mother

my desire is to preserve her in my mind,
make her live forever
and walk on all the footpaths of memory
as a denizen of a son's mind.

I want to feel her throwing me in the air,
lifting her eyes to follow my rise
and extending her arms timeously
to lock them under my fragile armpits
and break my descent to the ground.

I want to see her walking vigorously
my small fragile body strapped to her back
as I shift slowly
in rhythm with her body.

I want to see her hands
making circular motions on my body
soaping it with massaging gentleness
before cupping warm water all over it
and scooping me into the warmth of her bosom.

I want to see Mother in a floral dress
her vaselined skin glowing in the afternoon sun
a reverent look on her face
as she tugs me along to Sunday worship.

I want to see Mother sitting in the sun
chanting the prices of her wares to passers-by
and coaxing hard-headed ones to change their minds
and leave something to add to her small pile of coins.

I want to know how her skin became wrinkled
to painstakingly trace the creases on her face
mapping each line and dating it
until I understand the paths I have created on her face.

I want to preserve Mother in my mind
I want her to live forever
to traverse the footpaths of memory
until Memory and Mother become one.

Father

(to Munyaradzi Mudakuvaka)

I remember his voice flying in the moonlit night
heralding his arrival from a drinking stint in the next village
which necessitated two types of responses
that divided the homestead into two countries:
the delight of the dogs at hearing the master's arrival
and a funereal silence enveloping the kitchen hut,
everything scuttling for cover including the voices of the children.

Johwani fotini vhesi hwani
vhesi hwani
moyo yevatendi ngairege kumanikidzwa
tendaivo kuna baba
mutende nekwandri
vhesi hwani2

then a brief silence during which
he would probably be wondering whether to preach
or castigate the witches and phantoms that stood in his way
and fought against his progress in life.

I see Father staggering into the kitchen hut
and taking all outstanding issues head on
like why I was still clumsy with the plough
when Tavonga was already holding it with one hand
and directing the cattle with another,
or why Mother was in the habit of hiding his hard-earned coins
and depriving him of a few moments of joy with Chegovo and
company,
or why this regime of vegetables and sadza

---

2 This is a Christian chorus based on the words in John 14:1.

113

always coincidentally installed itself
on happy days like this one.

I hear Father's voice in the morning
summoning me to the cattle pen
to milk Butter, our very gentle cow3
who was always in the habit of throwing away all decorum
every time the process of milking involved me
so that one day, throwing all patience to the wind,
she pierced my Adidas shorts with her horn
and threw me into the air like a rag
to have me land accurately, and head first,
into the pail of milk that Father had coaxed from her breast.
I remember the day perfectly because the previous night
Father had come back home with another forehead on his head
and mumbled something about a fight involving himself and Sekuru4
Givhoti;
so for the pains of being thrown into the air by a gentle cow
I received a hiding
during which time I memorised the shape his face had taken
to assuage the pain that stung my bare backside.

I see Father raising a colossal building from the dust of the ground
uniting an army of bricks carefully
like a boy playing Sudoku with numerous pieces;
I hear him announcing that I had been recruited as a dhaka boy
and that I needed to learn a thing or two about building
who knows, maybe one day I would have to repair
the goat pen, or the fowl run;
I remember walking behind him to our new conquest,

---

3 Butter was the name of our only cow in the 90s and early 2000s.

4 Another word for 'Uncle'.

I remember hearing him barking instructions
about how to mix the ingredients
in order to have the perfect texture,
I hear him saying that I was good with books
but what was lacking was being good at other things
like mixing dhaka
or holding a plough
or milking Butter our gentle cow
or harnessing the cattle
or leading the cattle.

I remember Father moving to the city
to work as a bus driver,
I remember waking up every morning
with pride that somewhere in this country
my father was moving around a big machine
to the delight of his passengers.
I remember how the year Father moved to the city
Christmas came with a smile on its face,
there were new clothes that smelled of the city,
there were biscuits that he fished from a paper bag written OK on
the side
and there was sliced bread that looked different
from the clumsy chunks that we bought from the local shops.
I also remember Father building a new house of corrugated iron
and converting the thatched one into a storeroom.
I remember encouraging myself to grow up
and become a bus driver just like Father
and eat all the biscuits in the world
and build a bigger house for him and Mother
and more cattle and goats and chickens
and be a son he would be proud of.

I remember Father coming from the city in a wheelbarrow

'Accident!' was the whisper in the wind;
I remember his pained and vulnerable look
and how I had to hold him by the hand
or push him in a wheelbarrow,
how for months I prayed for him to walk again,
to drive again that big machine and bring biscuits and bread
and new clothes that smelled of the city;
I remember how he started to walk again,
tottering like a new-born calf
and sometimes landing on his buttocks after failing to brave the pain.

I remember Father coming to church
and telling the congregation that he was giving his life to God
and telling the shocked congregants
that it was God who had saved his life;
thereafter I see Father in a variety of postures:
in this one he is preaching about Paul and the Thessalonians
in that one he is holding a hymn book and fervently singing
Ndinosimuda She5
in yet another one he is in control of a funeral programme
and everyone is listening to him.

I see Father holding my new-born baby,
holding him closely to his chest with a lot of emotion,
scrutinising his face for a sign of himself:
a nose that stares down at the mouth maybe
or eyes that stare furtively at you while sizing you up with camera-
eye-precision.

I used to see Father every time I closed my eyes,
but these days, even without closing them, I see him
because I, too, have become a father.

---

5 This is a Christian hymn whose English version is 'I need thee Lord'.

memories
(to Leeroy Nyamande)

sometimes memories take you to a garden
where they hop from flower to flower
and linger momentarily where a flower's tit
is being suckled thoughtfully by an army of bees;
or they can drag you by the nose
to breathe in the surreal fragrance
of a flower during its happy moments.

then there are moments when memories
walk with you, chameleon-like,
through the valley of the shadow of death,
this dark tunnel in which everything is visible to the mind,
to make you trace with a sense of hopelessness
the inevitable pattern of your ending
which you have repeatedly seen being etched
on the bodies of those who have gone before you
but which appears new every time
because patterns of this nature are not meant to be understood.

I use my pen to laugh
cry
smile,
to scream that I am angry
sad
happy…

poetry

and these bones, strewn on the floor
of this yawning valley,
                    shall live again.

to write

to write is to sublimate experience into syntax,
to wrestle with ink and paper   .
until both become accomplices
in the creation of an abridged version
of this life that I live.

to write is to say:
when she kissed me
heaven and earth met for the first time
and the war between sea and land
came to a dramatic end.

words in flesh

take these sorrowful snippets
and rummage through them,
search for me in these verses
and leave my mind exposed in them,
pick my mind and prophesy
to these bones to live again,
then before your eyes I will stand,
vulnerable and open to your gaze
because "the word became flesh
and dwelled among men."

wounds

I curate my best wounds into poetry
and leave the worst ones as salt lines on the cheeks;
so we can safely say both the best and the worst
leave monuments behind:
syntactic lines for lips to kiss at every syllable
and salt lines for those who receive thrills
from gazing at lacerations left on withered cheeks.

even if my hope is like a mustard seed,
this mountain I will climb.

songs and dreams

my people love to sing,
to scribble graffiti
on the forehead of song,
to pick each bone from the throng
of dreams lying on the vast floor
of the twenty-first
and lyric them to life.

my people love to dance,
on dusty ground to prance
and leave behind footprints
of dreams that sprint
towards the horizon that hovers
beyond the mist of the twenty-first.

my people love to gaze at their dreams
rising like apparitions in the steam
of that euphoric November dance
that sets cold hearts ablaze
with anticipation for a more hopeful
journey along the paths of the twenty-first.

my people love to clothe dreams
in the stanzas and lyrics of song,
to let the dreams fly with sound
to come back as beautiful echoes
bouncing off the Chamavara range,
echoes of dreams and songs,
dreams, songs and people,
dreams, songs, people, the twenty-first.

peace

before this legion turmoil enters the Gadarene swine
this storm must not the saviour's voice spite.
my feet have attempted to defy the sinking sensation
that accompanies every step that I take
on the water's undulating passion
but only the hand that orders words into syntactic silence
can lead me towards the peace that hides in a denouement.

all poems are happy
(closing lines)

when my dreams fry under the 21st century sun,
when happiness my dark abode shuns,
when life's callous hands my tender heart shred,
when the stingy baobab hides its shade,
in my inkwell I will dip my quill.

when the voice of the praying saint becomes a sigh,
when the saviour tumbles out of his mother's womb in a pig sty,
when the preacher decides to read his bible backwards,
when the doctor poisons the patients in his ward,
in my inkwell I will dip my quill.

when Lucifer sits astride heavenway,
when my prayers disappear in Lucifer's stinking underwear,
when my fingers fail to grasp this skeleton,
of an impoverished and maimed revelation,
in my inkwell I will dip my quill.

when this sadness shrouds my spirit
like the fog of a season's end,
when all the happiness allocated to me is spent
and solitude's hold on me cannot relent,
in my inkwell I will dip my quill
and give to sadness a gentle thrill
because even if sadness is all we have left
I will still scratch and scream
rave and brave these nightmares of my existence
until life, tired of the noise,
finally smiles at me.

Publisher's list

If you have enjoyed *Because Sadness is Beautiful?*, consider these other fine books from Mwanaka Media and Publishing:

Cultural Hybridity and Fixity by Andrew Nyongesa
The Water Cycle by Andrew Nyongesa
Tintinnabulation of Literary Theory by Andrew Nyongesa
I Threw a Star in a Wine Glass by Fethi Sassi
South Africa and United Nations Peacekeeping Offensive Operations by Antonio Garcia
Africanization and Americanization Anthology Volume 1, Searching for Interracial, Interstitial, Intersectional and Interstates Meeting Spaces, Africa Vs North America by Tendai R Mwanaka
A Conversation..., A Contact by Tendai Rinos Mwanaka
A Dark Energy by Tendai Rinos Mwanaka
Africa, UK and Ireland: Writing Politics and Knowledge Production Vol 1 by Tendai R Mwanaka
Best New African Poets 2017 Anthology by Tendai R Mwanaka and Daniel Da Purificacao
Keys in the River: New and Collected Stories by Tendai Rinos Mwanaka
Logbook Written by a Drifter by Tendai Rinos Mwanaka
Mad Bob Republic: Bloodlines, Bile and a Crying Child by Tendai Rinos Mwanaka
How The Twins Grew Up/Makurire Akaita Mapatya by Milutin Djurickovic and Tendai Rinos Mwanaka
Writing Language, Culture and Development, Africa Vs Asia Vol 1 by Tendai R Mwanaka, Wanjohi wa Makokha and Upal Deb
Zimbolicious Poetry Vol 1 by Tendai R Mwanaka and Edward Dzonze

128

Zimbolicious: An Anthology of Zimbabwean Literature and Arts, Vol 3 by Tendai Mwanaka
Under The Steel Yoke by Jabulani Mzinyathi
A Case of Love and Hate by Chenjerai Mhondera
Epochs of Morning Light by Elena Botts
Fly in a Beehive by Thato Tshukudu
Bounding for Light by Richard Mbuthia
White Man Walking by John Eppel
A Cat and Mouse Affair by Bruno Shora
Sentiments by Jackson Matimba
Best New African Poets 2018 Anthology by Tendai R Mwanaka and Nsah Mala
Drawing Without Licence by Tendai R Mwanaka
Writing Grandmothers/ Escribiendo sobre nuestras raíces: Africa Vs Latin America Vol 2 by Tendai R Mwanaka and Felix Rodriguez
The Scholarship Girl by Abigail George
Words That Matter by Gerry Sikazwe
The Gods Sleep Through It by Wonder Guchu
The Ungendered by Delia Watterson
The Big Noise and Other Noises by Christopher Kudyahakudadirwe
Tiny Human Protection Agency by Megan Landman
Ghetto Symphony by Mandla Mavolwane
Sky for a Foreign Bird by Fethi Sassi
A Portrait of Defiance by Tendai Rinos Mwanaka
When Escape Becomes the only Lover by Tendai R Mwanaka
Where I Belong: moments, mist and song by Smeetha Bhoumik
Nationalism: (Mis)Understanding Donald Trump's Capitalism, Racism, Global Politics, International Trade and Media Wars, Africa Vs North America Vol 2 by Tendai R Mwanaka
Ashes by Ken Weene and Omar O Abdul

Ouafa and Thawra: About a Lover From Tunisia by Arturo Desimone
Thoughts Hunt The Loves/Pfungwa Dzinovhima Vadiwa by Jeton Kelmendi
ويَسهَرُ اللَّيلُ عَلَى شَفَتي...وَالغَمَام by Fethi Sassi
A Letter to the President by Mbizo Chirasha
Righteous Indignation by Jabulani Mzinyathi:
Blooming Cactus By Mikateko Mbambo
Phenomenology of Decolonizing the University: Essays in the Contemporary Thoughts of Afrikology by Zvikomborero Kapuya
Rhythm of Life by Olivia Ngozi Osouha
Travellers Gather Dust and Lust by Gabriel Awuah Mainoo

Soon to be released

Of Bloom Smoke by Abigail George
Denga reshiri yokunze kwenyika by Fethi Sassi
Notes From a Modern Chimurenga: Collected Stories by Tendai Rinos Mwanaka
Tom Boy by Megan Landman
My Spiritual Journey: A Study of the Emerald Tablets by Jonathan Thompson
School of Love and Other Stories by Ricardo Felix Rodriguez
Cycle of Life by Ikegwu Michael Chukwudi
INFLUENCE OF CLIMATE VARIABILITY ON THE PREVALENCE OF DENGUE FEVER IN MANDERA COUNTY, KENYA by NDIWA JOSEPH KIMTAI
Chitungwiza Mushamukuru Wakaenda Kupiko: An Anthology of Chitungwiza Writers and Artists by Tendai Rinos Mwanaka
Best New African Poets 2019 Anthology by Tendai Rinos Mwanaka and Nsah Mala